Contents

Some words are shown in bold, **like this**. You can find out what they mean by looking in the glossary.

What are masks and face painting?

Masks are objects that hide or protect a person's face.

Craftspeople all around the world make masks.

Start with Art

Masks and
Face Painting

Isabel Thomas

www.raintreepublishers.co.uk

Visit our website to find out more information about Raintree books.

To order:

☎ Phone 0845 6044371

▤ Fax +44 (0) 1865 312263

✉ Email myorders@raintreepublishers.co.uk

Customers from outside the UK please telephone +44 1865 312262

Raintree is an imprint of Capstone Global Library Limited, a company incorporated in England and Wales having its registered office at 7 Pilgrim Street, London, EC4V 6LB – Registered company number: 6695582

Edited by Dan Nunn, Rebecca Rissman, and Catherine Veitch
Designed by Richard Parker
Picture research by Mica Brancic and Hannah Taylor
Originated by Capstone Global Library
Printed and bound in China by South China Printing Company Ltd

ISBN 978 1 406 22739 0 (hardback)
15 14 13 12 11
10 9 8 7 6 5 4 3 2 1

ISBN 978 1 406 22742 0 (paperback)
16 15 14 13 12
10 9 8 7 6 5 4 3 2 1

British Library Cataloguing in Publication Data
Thomas, Isabel
Masks and face painting. -- (Start with art)
391.4'34-dc22
A full catalogue record for this book is available from the British Library.

Acknowledgements

We would like to thank the following for permission to reproduce photographs: Alamy Images pp. 7 (© Nikos Pavlakis), 13 (© PhotosIndia.com LLC), 14 (© Marli Wakeling), 19 (© Damian Tully); © Capstone Publishers pp. 11, 20, 21, 22, 23 – materials, 23 – papier mâché (Karon Dubke); Corbis pp. 8 (Richard T. Nowitz), 9 (Reuters/© Stringer Shanghai), 10 (© Charles & Josette Lenars); Getty Images p. 16 (The Image Bank/Penny Tweedie); iStockphoto pp. 17 (© Nina Shannon), 23 – craftspeople (© Karen Massier); Photolibrary p. 6 (Superstock); Shutterstock pp. 5, 23 – disguise, 23 – traditional (© Anna Omelchenko), 15 (© Tom Grundy), 18 (© Itinerant Lens), 23 – carved (© nagib), 23 – mosaic (© tratong); The Art Archive p. 4 (National Anthropological Museum Mexico/Dagli Orti); The Bridgeman Art Library p. 12.

Front cover photograph of a Hulit tribesman, Papua New Guinea reproduced with permission of Corbis (© Bob Krist). Back cover photograph of papier mâché making reproduced with permission of © Capstone Publishers (Karon Dubke). Back cover photograph of a zebra mask reproduced with permission of Shutterstock (© Tom Grundy).

Every effort has been made to contact copyright holders of material reproduced in this book. Any omissions will be rectified in subsequent printings if notice is given to the publisher.

All the Internet addresses (URLs) given in this book were valid at the time of going to press. However, due to the dynamic nature of the Internet, some addresses may have changed, or sites may have changed or ceased to exist since publication. While the author and publisher regret any inconvenience this can cause readers, no responsibility for any such changes can be accepted by either the author or the publisher.

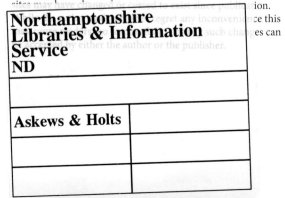

People can also **disguise** their faces with paints.

Masks and face painting are some of the oldest types of art.

Where can I see masks and face painting?

Celebrations and festivals are good places to see masks and face painting.

This person has a painted face to celebrate a carnival.

Museums collect masks from different times and places for everyone to see.

Visit a museum to get ideas for making your own masks.

What do people use to make masks?

Some masks are made from hard **materials**, such as wood and metal.

This gold mask is **500** years old. It was made to last a long time.

People sometimes make masks out of **papier mâché**.

These children have made masks to celebrate Chinese New Year.

How do people make masks?

African masks are often **carved** out of wood.

People paint or carve shapes and patterns on to the wood.

This girl is making a mask using **papier mâché**.

When the paper dries it will be hard and strong.

Why do people wear masks and paint their faces?

Some masks are made to be worn on special occasions such as ceremonies.

People wear the masks to bring good luck.

People often **disguise** their faces to tell stories.

This actor is performing in a play in India.

What can masks show?

A mask can show the face of a person.

It might be someone who lived long ago, or a person from a story.

Animal masks can have special meanings.

This mask is shaped like a zebra's head.

What can face painting show?

In some places, people paint their faces with **traditional** patterns.

This boy in Australia is taking part in a special ceremony.

Face painting can change you into somebody or something else.

This girl is pretending to be a tiger.

How do masks and face paints make us feel?

Masks and face paints change the way a person looks.

This red ogre mask makes the actor look scary.

Celebration masks are bright and colourful.

This carnival mask makes us feel happy.

Start to make masks!

The mask on page 4 was made by people called Aztecs. Try making your own **mosaic** mask.

1. Use a thick black pen to draw a mouth, teeth, and eyes on a white paper plate.

2. Cut the top off the plate to make a head shape.

3. Cut out lots of little squares from blue paper. Use different shades of blue.

4. Use glue to stick the paper squares to the mask.

5. Ask a grown-up to cut holes for your eyes and fix elastic to your mask.

6. Now you can wear your Aztec mask!

Glossary

carved made using a cutting tool to shape a hard material, such as wood

craftspeople people who make arts and crafts

disguise change how something looks

materials things you can use to make art

mosaic design made by sticking many small coloured squares together

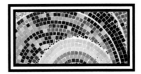

papier mâché way to make models by sticking pieces of paper over a shape in layers

traditional something that has been done in a special way for a very long time

Find out more

Books

Art to Make You Scared, Elizabeth Newbury (Frances Lincoln, 2007)

Super Simple Masks: Fun and Easy-to-Make Crafts for Kids, Karen Latchana Kenney (Abdo Publishing Company, 2009)

Websites

Make a mask based on famous art at this website: kids.tate.org.uk/create/make-a-mask.shtm

Visit this website to explore masks of the world: www.imagine.org.uk/adventure/masks/flash.php?file=maskPreloader&bypass=true

Index